La Belle Dame

Tom Carlson

Gordon Osing

Spuyten Duyvil Limited Editions
New York City

Poems and text ©2012 Gordon Osing
Collage art ©2012 Tom Carlson
ISBN 978-1-881471-00-4

Library of Congress Cataloging-in-Publication Data

Osing, Gordon, 1937-
La belle dame / Gordon Osing, Tom Carlson.
p. cm.
ISBN 978-1-881471-00-4
I. Carlson, Tom, 1944- II. Title.
PS3565.S56B45 2012
811'.54--dc23
2011049170

for Sue and M.J.

And shall we call her whiter than the snow?
Sprayed first with ruby, then with emerald sheen—
Least tearful and least glad (who knows her smile?)
A caught slide shows her sandstone grey between.
Her eyes exist in swivellings of her teats,
Pearls whip her hips, a drench of whirling strands.
Her silly snake rings begin to mount, surmount
Each other—turquoise fakes on tinseled hands.

Hart Crane, "The Bridge"

"Vices enter into the makeup of virtues, just as poisons in the makeup of medicines. Prudence unites them, tempers them, and makes use of them against the ills of life," wrote La Rouchefoucauld (Maxim 182), and so gives us a glass through which to see doubly the ladies of French postcards and of the cabarets a hundred-and-fifty years ago. They are famous enough in the paintings of Degas and Lautrec to be sure, with the dark tophats and canes shadowed in the work, but we do not hear them speak about their chances perforce performed for these chaps. They seem to wear the female costumes of the minds of men, of ancient goddesses in *tableaux vivants* and high-kicking lines in the Moulin Rouge, semi-clad on bicycles, on the feminine pedestals in men's minds, justified by men's exaggerations, for all their plumages and feathers and sequins posings as suggestive *majas*. And what would one of them say, as we grant her an audience? Let us grant her prudence with a shrewd tongue.

LA BELLE DAME

His butterfly he calls me, his beauty,
his life overrun with duty, his garden
my self for his dalliances from necessities.
We daughters, sisters, mothers—know otherwise
whose necessaries are being pigeon-holed.
In their shattered mirror we are obliged
to see ourselves. Ours, it seems, is to put down
visible tracks from their solemn beings to
their less than secret pleasures, which, who
doesn't know all about. The right eye cannot
but know what the left is seeing. Eyes
share time, the moments if not the years.
Is one silent so the other sees? No,
I think not. So how can we share time?
Not if we are to be crucified wagging
our legs up over the lights and holding
a costumed pose to be all their mirrors
and veils, only one of our nine lives,
cats, not butterflies. Must we always give
what they say they cause in us, bring out,
our true lives before god? *Don Juans*
they are who must first degrade
what they say they cannot help but love.

PRY us from our secrets if you can, or force
us to give up or abandon our true lives;
they won't see what they'll get until they do.
They'll not get even one of our nine lives,
but their own words mocking themselves.
It is themselves they are paying to possess,
their money not the last of their indecencies.
Why must we always give their faces lips,
serve them that trifle ourselves, their words
slithering in our skin, as in Eden, where
once and always we together fall.

THEY gossip about a girl's ecstasies
they caused, over brandies, that fine ladies
choose not to allow, for it amounts to surrender
to his beliefs about his God-given self.
Acting is little known to him. Country girls
and always from other towns know better
when they soon enough go knees and toes
circling on stage and leaving the crowds
on an arm for what's left of the evening.
Their manhood lives in our pleasure, so
why not sell it to them. Nothing's free.
What else have we got to sell? The naïve
among us are the most to be pitied.
The best may get a better place, in *Clichy*.

PRIEST says my silence is the perfect part
of His humiliation. The Savior's I mean.
My job is pondering in the Holy Book,
weeping near the cross eventually. Vanity
is made to be turned inside out in us.
Our best defense is silent suffering.
Even if it is our heart he panders
and we tire profoundly of being his
sexual clown. Lautrec says yesterday
one is free only in art. A pity it is
seeming is the best of ours. Truly I
might have been more persons than
he has fingers if his darkest need
is for our being the needful *mademoiselle*.

Ours are saints' stories, except martyrs
to manhood, in bistros, in cheap hotels.
After devotion to God and their money, they
come around for their rewards, our selves.
Notres Dames. Indulgences in the boudoir.
Confession back stage, absolution by the hour,
and penance in pleasurable weariness home.
Brandy and cigars with the boys at the club.
One helluva Heaven they find in our embraces.
They have hunted the King's deer, the forbidden
one with King's cross on his head, held high
between the antlers, in the cheap tiara
we wear on our heads, for the Holy Ghost
exotic birds, sequins and dyed feathers.

THEY don't know a pedestal from a tombstone
(and they love only both) where under
and upon only they allow us to exist,
their mothers' unlikes. Who wins when
love is merely a fool's need. They laugh
only to see our self-abandonment,
our playing the courtesan, except they
are not *chevaliers*, not by a long shot.
They make a living selling each other
the shit of the good life, whatever that is.
I know what that is; it is freedom from
the judgments of those who have less,
or more, a good deal more, no end to it.
We laugh at and pity them to our own cost.

FUNNY it is the way they believe
they choose one of us, who are themselves
the chosen. Their shadows in and out of
the lamps backstage are to us more real
than they are if their need is hardly secret.
Daddies they want to be, us for children
flowering naughtily in their gardens of money.
Nobodaddies is what they really are.
They are moved only by our surrender,
to pouches of money hidden in their pants.
Their need is to escape their religion of bodies,
through a comedy of pleasure in ours.
They come for us in the nights of their beings.
In our legs smiling they dodge the world.

Mon dieu, how they love our stage lamps,
believed in same as the heavens as property,
with our little girl smiles as mirrors, amused
at how clever is everything they say. We
don't mind the games in it, nor even worlds
between theirs and ours. Life may well be
a sport and a pastime, as the wise have said,
but so are flowers, soups, paintings, and breads
for which love both kills and raises the dead.
They're not as far apart as hims and hers.
The hats go back to their wives and children,
and the more's the pity on them. I say
cast a pearl into your cup of wine.
We have it truer than they'll ever find.

Or did you want verses to say all this?
Cupid throws the biggest rock he can
into the smallest pond, the grace they pretend.
And people take us home in their luggage
and Paris lives on their nightstand. The awful
truth is understood, memorized if need be.
Most nights we sing as best we can, dance
and jump around or form into *tableaux vivants*,
and desire is made exciting by the mere possibility
of having pretended theatrically to men's
palavering. Like opera and paintings only belied,
if you know what I mean. *Tableaux erotiques*,
formed hurriedly to a frieze of almost bodies.
Why not perfect what you make a living doing.

PERFECTLY sacrificing love doesn't need
evidence or proof or even an object.
The first step of resistance we say is
some, any, life that is a real, working life.
Jesus, the wordless Word, loves everybody.
The rock of mercy is not money, even if
lots of us don't mind a *franc* or two.
Look at me, holding on to god knows what,
his proclamations over my privates. Only
falsely can we be seen otherwise if
we don't give them their language.
They come to us as if our need were
the matter. Who is the wanton here,
whose company is sold by the evening?

Who rocked thee, not my cradle in that gracious
        spot,
That garden of the happy, where heaven en-

R.   s thee

"INNOCENT CHILD AND SNOW WHITE
        FLOWER."

INNOCENT child and snow white flower!
Well are ye paired in your opening hour
Thus should the pure and the lovely meet,
Stainless with stainless, and sweet with sweet.

White as those leaves, just blown apart,
Are the folds of thy own young heart;
Guilty passion and cankering care,
Never have left their traces there.

Artless one! though thou gazest now
On the white blossom with earnest brow,
Soon will it tire thy childish eye,
Fair as it is, thou wilt throw it by.

Throw it aside in thy weary hour,
Throw to the ground the fair white flower,
Yet, as thy tender years depart,
Keep that fair and innocent heart.

THEY scarcely listen when we talk.
What we have is their language turned
on itself. Our job is to make it bawdily
attractive. The truth is every word
in every language is in our bodies.
If we are not the true silent word
I'll eat my hat, we'll, ours. *Mon dieu*,
he thinks his *pego* is a birthright.
A puissant regal good life he wants,
a life that lacks a comedy of itself,
as if the Devil invented laughter,
and so what if he did and it betrays
every single sacred doctrine of men.
The Devil's side is hardly all bad.

THEY look at us but they do not see.
Desire to be possessed by God's love
is to them the same as ours paid for.
We are creation's bright birds tamed,
pleasure in Heaven realized on earth.
Do not the stars come out to play
every night. Stage lamps and sequins shine,
savage feathers and jeweled tiaras make
any of us Sheba. "Solomon in all his glory…"
Paradise is when we open our faces and
make them men. They drink to our powers
of forgetting. Time's a fool anyway,
pleasure a fifth estate, a raw politics
whose object is prettier than wedding cake.

Does desire belong to god? *Peut-etre,*
peut-etre que non. What is desire among
the animals? Is not the jungle sacred also?
God made it. Would you convict a tiger
for being hungry? One's being is the same
as having one's way isn't it? We don't mind
being Eve puffed up in the Garden of Eden,
imitating the flowers, the birds, the sparkling
streams. Let that be one of our lives.
The shame is that men come to buy it,
not just to enjoy but to pay for it.
It is each other they want secretly.
Only priests are worse, who preach
flesh dissolved. Save that for the death-bed.

WHEN did we become the faces, Jesus's,
taking away the sins of the world? Cannibal
smiles of blameless desire size us up, ours
happily empty, to be filled, primal caves,
caverns, in lieu of everything on earth.
Mon dieu—but I forget, all their hymns
are to a Him. We are, apparently, to be
the decoration on top of Solomon's thousand
wedding cakes. As if that one life could
be enough, is for the likes of us. His
money our pleasure, thank you. Favorite
old clothes on a chilly morning are better.
Vegetable gardens, not His Eden. Ours. I wonder
who it was taught cannibals to just kiss.

WHO could begin to see herself
as men do? Who would want to,
but for an advantage in it and then
know nothing else. They caress the tops
of their canes and push their top hats
back or down on their heads and
lick their lips and take their measure
of us and we are expected to wait
at the back door of the stage for
their least or most compelling interest
and live by it either way. Hold a pose
until they have gazed long enough
to get past the silliness we represent,
pretending to be ancient statues. Their
need a virile virtue in pretending.

IT'S nothing but work being their butterflies.
We are young, young, young until
we are not. We are obliged to imagine,
no, pretend—everything. And then some.
And wait upon them to see what comfort
comes our way. Money's not the worst.
We give them the whole of life, they
give us what they must. We make right,
no, righteous their manly powers. Talk
about *droit du seigneur*. Still happening
it is, only under the weight of the necessary.
What are they looking for, sincerity?
No, desperation grown routine, capable
of holding a pose, all but perfecting an act.

COME on in. We are the city dancing
away your cares, the city of youth
and youth mocks old words as much as
anything. It's like a religion of the city
how they love us, and try to have us
by the rules, and love us for them.
We are the only city of real believing.
What do they not haunt in us? With their
naughty cant. They can exaggerate anything.
Hold it to an image. In an avenue shop
a gal can have her pick of the lords
in their castles, themselves, upright men,
if you don't mind the joke of that.
They adore the sin of making love.
Make it a god frightened by privilege.
Own us in *tableaux* then. Purchase
us in corner *tabacs* to pack for travel.
Stare up at the lighted stage where we
kick higher as the night goes on.
Catholic boys staring at the silver sacrament.

It strands desire in time to believe
pleasure proves something of the spiritual.
But we're a Catholic town, lights,
theatre and all. We are pure models
of men protesting their sins decently.
After all, we who do this work have
belonged to our kind since Eden's briars,
themselves made to clear thorns and tares,
to come sweating in to the girl in the house.
To hear her bear children in ultimate
pain. No wonder Sarah laughed.
I guess Abraham thought it was her due.
What's the city for if not orphans in time,
of the canes and top hats, of our blood.

And now
Miss Yvette
Guilbert
will sing "Le Roi Renard"

THE serpent, us talking to ourselves,
only whispered what we already knew.
Men's piety is as bad as their sting.
You'd think we are entirely on their side
of the fence, making it easy for them.
It's alright; the two ends of railroad
tracks never happen. (Do I tell them that?)
Men mislay desire easy as a wrench.
They try to play tennis on both sides
of the net; we are the net. Even
the gentlest mockery fails when they stand
in the waxing and waning moonlight.
No matter to us their worldly sultanships.
Who wants to be a *Moliere* of Methodists.

TO THE FRINGED GENTIAN.

lossom, igh autum
red wi he ven's o
nest, when the quiet li
the keen and frosty ni

est not when violet,
ering brooks and s
nes, in purple dre
he ground b d's hi

est late, and om'st al
ods re bare the birds
and rtenin days j
yea ea his en

AND do we have to know what we're doing
to be doing it? Of course not. Simply, better
this theatre than unicorns, tantalists of olden
times, when mystical creatures didn't screw.
Ours is the bawdy, ancient comedy of desire
still surviving in cabarets, in paid singers
charged by desire into perfect song, like
an emperor's canary. Songs wavering
to perfection, strong with singing, gayly
defiant. Pulsing with experience wagered.
And not, but just tired of the same games
and still wanting them. "No Regrets"
let one of us sing, and of roses opening.
Who knows, love happens anywhere.

THE bouquets of desire in men's minds:
it's a living. It might even lead to love,
good as anyway. Once in so many nights.
The top hats: I'll bet their wives at last
are glad they are here, not home longing.
Here in the cabaret we see their mouths gazing,
licking their lips, disguising hard, infantile
eyes. Rubbing the knobs of their canes.
Guilty monkeys they all are, wanting both
the sin and their righteousness before it,
their need forgiven and ours patronized.
Worse luck befalls the ones who fall in love
with one of us. She knows his love
for the one at home will turn pure duty.

Remove all definite
lines and you will
see the thing itself
not a thing but a
moment a definite
instance, a trivial
miracle or mystery
wherein the eye
drowns willingly
if it can
The eye is a clock
made of water

WHAT else am I willing to do? Who can
deny the truth of a photograph. Ancient
statues show no more or less. I think
they call it classical art; the joke's on them.
Extra money for randy pictures for men
needing dark to cover their desire hiding
in the *camera obscura* with the powders.
Daguerrotypes have come a long way
since our shadows captured on glass panes.
Boys will be boys, they say. Their mothers
are to be commended. Teach them to lie
like photographs, not stutter, and swallow honor.
Theirs it is to brag to each other, their
desires not as single as they think.

WE are the *harim* in their fashioned minds.
Their Bible confirms we brought down
the world into thistles and tares, and they
are entitled to our penalty at it forever.
They save us by their humored desire,
when it is given to having its way. Even then,
the sin is ours with the grace it allays.
Only that our pleasure at their hands
be given, as if we had no choice.
Our pleasure is the coin of their lands.
The worst among them know when it is real.
We make them real as pockets of money,
moreover, get hands out of pockets, forgiving
both purses and manhood hanging there.

〜CIAN'S COUNSELS TO WO〜

We shall proceed to answer in detail the quest〜 What makes woma〜

Her Form.

〜his is characteristic even at a 〜ry early age. A certain gracefulness of outline is everywhere observable. The bone〜 lighter and smaller than in the〜 sex. The collar-bone is longer 〜 curved. The lower limbs are set 〜 apart 〜 which results a peculia〜 gait. 〜s are broader, so as to give a 〜 e to that band of bone which 〜 organs destined for maternity. Th〜 〜omical differences are shadowed forth even in early girlhood; they become more marked as the age of puberty draws nigh; and they 〜re fully es〜hed at maturity.

The muscu〜 system is 〜so less developed in the girl than in the boy.

NOBODY'S daughters, mothers, sisters,
ours is the burden of their desires to be
worldly. Our hearts are rewarded by those
who pay their ways into---our hearts,
if you can believe anything they pretend.
Apaches out back at the stage door
are no better and no worse, but broke
often enough not to be regular fare.
The top hats want us for a while,
twirling our legs or posing Aphrodites
with empty faces until and unless
Cupid smiles and our music blares
and they want what they want in us.
Organ grinders' monkeys are as well off
as we. They have as many years to ply
their trade of proffering and begging,
and they cannibal a banana the same as we.

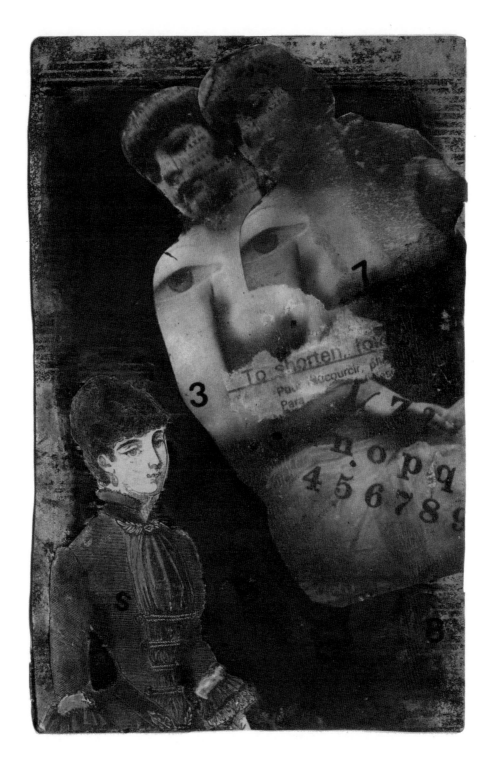

WHY must one always suspect serious men
of having put off what they want most?
Games of love and our bellies in our minds.
Why do they think if they pay, laughter
and singing and dancing and games of the *boudoir*
can be had by compensated blame. Why do we
agree to it, unless their words, plastered
on our skins, say it has to be so. Priests
forgive it all the time, so it's a rule.
And god knows, money and sex and God
are the same thing in our juggling hands.
The top and the bottom know the same;
it's the fops in the middle that are not
allowed, really, to believe or know anything
but how to get to the next step in pretending.
They have their theatre, god help us all.

ENCORE

WHAT we know every moon takes
them a lifetime to learn, if ever:
blood sacrifice is the heart of any
real religion, as the whole world knows;
it's just them and their doctrines that don't.
Men offer up their own sons to man-language,
put off the knife so that their god intervenes,
approving. They present a language maniac
with system and unarguable definitions,
that make them like their god, themselves,
that rule behind the altar not on it, where
the knife is always raised to a death
not their own but guarding their gender
against us full of them in our blood.

GORDON OSING is retired from the writing program at the University of Memphis and lives now lakeside in Delta bluffs woods in Eudora, Mississippi, where he is continuing his career in reading and writing and traveling. The River City Writers Series, that he began some thirty-five years ago at the University of Memphis, is still thriving. He sees himself in a continuation of the works of the Southern Modernists, holding language in poetry as re-contextualized, and the poem as artifact with its own protocols and reasons, the ways and means of a poem's attachments to "truth" belonging peculiarly to poetry.

TOM CARLSON taught American literature and creative nonfiction at the University of Memphis for thirty-two years. He has published extensively on Melville, Poe, eastern European poetry, and American popular culture.

Made in the USA
Charleston, SC
04 April 2012